MW01173132

The Veteran Workbook

The tool to help you reflect on your service and design your future,
by building structure and re-defining who you are today.

This book belongs to _____

If found, please contact _____

Copyright © 2023 by Jenna L. Carlton

This workbook may bring up some
tough emotions or memories.
Please know you are never alone.
Help is always available.

Suicide and Crisis Lifeline number: 988 press 1

CONTENTS

Introduction

No matter how long you served or how long it has been since you left the military, this workbook is for you. In this book, there are a total of 42 themes that fall into 4 categories. Each category is meant to guide you to either: set up structure, re-define your most authentic self, reflect on your time in service, or plan for the future.

This book is designed so you don't have to go in order. Whatever you feel you need to work on or if something sounds interesting, go ahead and start there. It is also set up so you can work at your own pace. There is no fixed amount of time in which you need to complete each theme, however it is recommended to do one set of questions a day.

The Categories

Structure

The military told us where to be, when to be there, and how to look when you show up. Leaving the military puts the power back in our hands to create our own life. The time is now to decide what you want out of this next adventure in life, and to build the foundation that will help you sustain it. This category will help you see where you can set yourself up, so your life is matching your intentions.

Re-define Yourself

Getting out of the military is leaving an entire culture behind. Veterans often feel lost after service and unsure of who they are. Your job in the military was interwoven into so many aspects of your life, it became part of your identity. Now as a civilian, it is time to re-define who you are without the military. This doesn't mean going back to who you were before the military. You have changed and grown in so many ways. This category is going to help you define exactly who you are and how to be your most confident self.

Reflection of Service

You have been through a lot while serving. This category helps you take a step back and process everything you have experienced while in uniform. It may not be comfortable, but it is necessary in moving forward in life. A lot has changed since you first signed your life away. It is important to check in with how you feel about your service now that you have a chance to look at it in retrospect.

Planning for the Future

In uniform, your future wasn't always in your hands. It was hard to plan for something you felt was out of your control. Now as a civilian, you may be able to have more control of where life takes you. This category will help you recognize what you need to do to set yourself up for the future you envision.

The Veteran Workbook

Theme 1:
Making Space

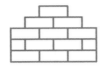

You will be more likely to work on this workbook if you carve out a specific time and space to do it. Think of a time of day where writing will be easy and you will have few distractions. Perhaps in your car before you go into work, right before you go to sleep, or while on lunch break. Try to pick a time that will be consistent.

1. Make space for the life you want. Today is the foundation of your journey. Making space to dedicate to yourself everyday is so important. Throughout the day, you may notice a few moments where you can linger a little longer.

Where did you find space for yourself today?

What does it feel like to have time dedicated to just you?

2. Success isn't made by what you do every once in a while. The only promised way to grow is by being consistent.

Creating space may be difficult at first, but slowly it becomes a part of your routine. Being consistent will help you form a routine that comes automatically. In the past, what has your relationship with consistency been like?

How can being consistent change your life?

3. Reflection Day:

What are you grateful for today?

[ ]

What was your favorite part of the day?

[ ]

What are you looking forward to?

[ ]

4. Get into the habit of asking yourself:
"Does this support the life I'm trying to create?"

What are some of your good habits?

[ ]

What are some you want to get rid of?

[ ]

5. Whatever you are currently doing consistently should look like the future you are dreaming of.

Where did you notice some extra time today?

How can you set yourself up for a better day tomorrow?

6. Check-in Day:

How are you doing?

What has been working out for you?

What changes have you noticed?

4

Theme 2:
Keeping a Promise to Yourself

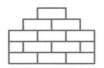

When you started this workbook, you made a promise to yourself, of a better life after service. Keeping this promise not only honors your present self, but sets your future self up for success. Remember this promise whenever you have wavering thoughts about your journey.

1. Keeping promises to yourself is the highest form of self love.

How have you let yourself down in the past?

What promises do you currently have with yourself?

2. Trusting yourself is the key to personal growth

What can you promise to yourself today, that you can fulfill tomorrow?

How has your mental health been lately?

3. Reflection Day:

What are you grateful for today?

What was your favorite part of the day?

What are you looking forward to?

4. Once upon a time you were a small child with dreams that you promised yourself you would make real. While they weren't always practical, they did bring you joy at one point?

How did you picture your adult life when you were a child?

What happened today that was special?

5. "The only person you are destined to become is the person you decide to be." -Ralph Waldo Emerson

What was it that impacted you, that helped you decide what you want in life?

What is something that has taken your breath away?

6. Check-in Day:

How are you doing?

What has been working out for you?

What changes have you noticed?

Theme 3:
Identity Crisis

When you get out of the military, you have to re-discover yourself without the military. This can be frustrating because most of us were teenagers when we joined and reverting back to that persona may not be the best choice. You've been told how to dress and how to groom for the last however many years. The military also has its own culture (lingo, mannerisms, expectations) that doesn't always fit in with the civilian world you are now a part of. It's hard to integrate back to regular life without being frustrated or feeling like you don't belong. You absolutely do belong. The key is to re-learn yourself without the military. Go easy on yourself because this can take years. During this theme we are going to focus on how to find your genuine self, post-military.

1. In the military we didn't have to overthink what we were going to wear. Your personal style may now be coming into question.

What clothes/colors make you feel most confident and why?

How has your style changed throughout the years?

2. We all have moments where we feel we are being judged. Entering back into civilian life can make us think twice about how others perceive us.

Have you ever felt like you stood out like a sore thumb? Explain

What do you wish others knew about you?

3. Reflection Day:

What are you grateful for today?

What was your favorite part of the day?

What are you looking forward to?

4. Dissociating from the military is also very common when you first get out. We can now indulge in styles that we weren't able to before (beards/colored hair).

What did you look forward to being able to do when you got out?

How has not having to be in regulations changed your appearance?

5. Being in the military gives you an automatic sense of pride in your job (or at least the majority of the public views it that way). You may not have that with whatever you are pursuing in the civilian world, but that doesn't mean it is any less important.

How are you continuing to serve others in your daily life?

How can you find importance in your current role?

6. Check-in Day:

How are you doing?

What has been working out for you?

What changes have you noticed?

Theme 4:
Taking Back Control of Your Future

The military had almost total control of our lives. We didn't have much choice as to where we would be living or for how long. Since so many choices were made for us, it can be overwhelming at how many choices we now have. You may even avoid decisions about the future because they seem intimidating and sometimes unnatural. You have done so much reflection thus far, let's see how we can apply that into your future decisions.

1. Being contract free, your future is officially in your hands.

If you had not joined the military, what were your plans?
What would you have done instead?

What do you have to take into consideration while planning for your future?

2. In the military, it could sometimes feel pointless to make future plans because they could be changed in an instant due to the needs of the mission. Here is your permission to get excited about your future again!

What plans did you avoid making due to being in the military?

What plans have you made or do you want to make that excite you about your future career or a life goal?

3. Reflection Day:

What are you grateful for today?

What was your favorite part of the day?

What are you looking forward to?

4. You now have more control over your medical and dental needs. You are now solely responsible for keeping up with your health.

How have you ensured your health needs are being met?

Is there anything stopping you from seeking care? What are possible solutions?

5. Your financial needs were 'mostly' in your hands when you served. Now in the civilian world, you may no longer have that safety net the military provides.

How has your relationship with money been?

What do you need to do to ensure you will be okay financially?

6. Check-in Day:

How are you doing?

What has been working out for you?

What changes have you noticed?

Theme 5: Accountability

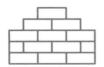

    Scary news: You're on your own now. But also, good news: You are on your own now! While we were in we had a set of rules that legally held us accountable if we were involved in misconduct. We were motivated to uphold certain values by having serious consequences. In the civilian world we don't have such harsh repercussions. We are now responsible for setting our own boundaries on what we feel is of our morals or character. You now have the opportunity to be motivated by love instead of fear. This theme will set you up with how you can hold yourself responsible in a caring way.

1. One of the greatest forms of self love is calling yourself out on behavior that doesn't align with who you want to be.

In what ways do you currently hold yourself responsible?

What is something that feels like self love, but by indulging too much, can actually be self harm?

2. We play the biggest role in how our life unfolds. Looking in the mirror is uncomfortable, but essential to growth.

How are you playing a role in your own suffering?

In what ways have you been brutally honest with yourself in the past?

3. Reflection Day:

What are you grateful for today?

What was your favorite part of the day?

What are you looking forward to?

4. You are not responsible for what happens to you in life, however you are responsible for how you respond.

How have you mistakenly put the blame on outside sources when you were truly at fault?

How have you put the blame on yourself when it was completely out of your control?

5. Social norms and culture may make us feel an automatic responsibility for things that you actually had no control over. It is important to question why you feel responsible. Below, reflect on relationships, obligations to work or others, and family dynamics.

Here's a chart to draw a clear line.

What I am responsible for:	What I am not responsible for:

6. Check-in Day:

How are you doing?

What has been working out for you?

What changes have you noticed?

20

Theme 6:
Forgive Yourself

"The relationship you have with yourself is the most complicated because you can't walk away from you. You have to forgive every mistake and deal with every flaw. You have to find a way to love you even when you are disgusted with you." -Unknown

We are all human. We all try to act the best way we can with the information and experience we had in that moment. It is time to give yourself grace for past versions of yourself. That is all we really can do with the past, make peace of it, learn from it, and move on. We need to actively forgive ourselves and acknowledge that we did the best we could. While working through this theme you are going to reflect on your past self and make some needed peace so you don't have to carry it with you anymore.

1. Forgive yourself for not having your current future in mind, because what seems obvious now, was once never possible.

Write down the biggest mistake you've made in the past and then describe your thought process behind this mistake. How can you give yourself grace for this past moment?

What are some past choices you have now forgiven yourself for?

2. Every choice you've made, whether you regret it or not, has brought you to this very moment.

What is a "bad" choice you made that turned out for the better?

How have you been grateful for your past bad decisions?

3. Reflection Day:

What are you grateful for today?

What was your favorite part of the day?

What are you looking forward to?

4. Forgiving your past self is a gift your present self can give to your future self.

If you could free yourself of any past guilt, what would it be and why?

How have others forgiven your past actions?

5. Let go of your past and give yourself permission to move forward.

Why are you still holding on to past mistakes?

What would it be like to move forward, completely at peace with your past?

6. Check-in Day:

How are you doing?

What has been working out for you?

What changes have you noticed?

Theme 7:
Defining Your Values

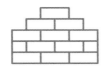

We were given values to uphold when we signed our life away in service of our country. However great those may be, we need to define our own personal values. When circumstances in life change, your values are bound to change as well. For this theme you will be checking in on your values so you have a clear direction of where to put your efforts. Most of us have common values, but depending on your place in life you may find worth in different areas. It is important to be honest with yourself and truly reflect on what you value.

1. Values are the things you consider to give meaning to your life. Without them, you do not have direction.

What gives meaning to your life?

What is something that keeps you going every day?

2. Values are personal. We find ourselves being frustrated when our values are not understood. Think about arguments you have had in the past. There was most likely either an unequal understanding of values or each person had different values that caused the disagreement.

Reflect on a time when your values were misunderstood. How did this come about?

How can you live your life so your values are always at the forefront of your intentions?

3. Reflection Day:

What are you grateful for today?

What was your favorite part of the day?

What are you looking forward to?

4. Values are our guides. We tend to be drawn to people with similar values and look for partners who live out those same values.

Who is in your life right now simply because you share a value?

How has an unshared value ended a friendship/relationship you were in?

5. Being authentic with yourself is the best way to find your values. It is okay for them to be different then what they were years ago. Our circumstances change and therefore our values do. For example, most young people value being social and outgoing. As they get older they may value self-care and family more. Think about what you want to honor in your life.

Reflect on who you were five years ago. What did you value then? Do you still value it now? Why or why not?

How do you think your values will change in the future?

6. Check-in Day:

How are you doing?

What has been working out for you?

What changes have you noticed?

7. Communicating our values is so important to feeling accepted and respected in our communities. When our partner, parents, or children know what we value, they will begin to understand us more. For example, you may really value being on time for events. You can communicate this value with friends and family by planning ahead and making sure meeting a timeframe is achievable.

How can you communicate your value to those around you?

Think of a time you told someone about something you value. How did they respond?

Theme 8:
The Significance of Routine

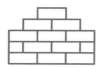

Routine is second nature in the military. Routine was for the most part out of our control. Out of the military, our routine could be more flexible and something we can tailor to our needs and goals. Now that you have taken a look at all the habits you want to limit, let's put those extra resources to good use. The secret of your future is woven into your daily routine. The small things you do every day add up to become the person you want to be. Adding things to your routine are specific to you and can be used to reach any goals you have (ex: health goals, career goals, etc.)

1. Being consistent is more valuable than being great every once in a while. Think of your friends and family. Would you rather them show up when you needed them to or them show up every once in a while and bring a gift. The gift probably is meaningless because you appreciate them being there for you over anything else. Treat your habits the same. Showing up every day, even if you aren't doing your best, is still better than not showing up at all.

What is an example of a time you skipped out on something because you thought you wouldn't be your best? (Being mentally or physically ill doesn't count.)

How has someone showing up for you made you feel?

2. "Routine is boring" …said someone who doesn't stick to a routine. Think of a routine as a scaffolding to your life. It is merely the structure to which you can add or remove whatever you please. It is a forever evolving schedule that will grow with you and your values. Make it fun, make it fabulous!

What part of your current routine excites you?

How can you add a little bit of spice into your routine tomorrow?

3. Reflection Day:

What are you grateful for today?

What was your favorite part of the day?

What are you looking forward to?

4. Think of your routine as a series of values you are living out each day. Focus on the broad meaning of each step to a routine instead of the minor details. Here's an example. If your routine is to walk each day in the morning, but it is raining out today so you can't. Don't skip the step, re-work it. Think about what you get most out of your goal. If your intention of walking is centered around clearing your mind, try meditating instead. Or if your intention is to be more active, try doing some chores that would be equally as exerting. Apply this process anytime a hiccup comes up in routine.

List the values your routine embodies.

How has your routine changed with your values over time?

5. Inspiration and motivation come and go, but routine is something you can depend on. No one wakes up every day inspired, but that doesn't mean they can't get things done. Sometimes all it takes is a good routine and the confidence in knowing that you are building a better life.

What goals are you able to work on daily? Weekly?

How have you gotten through a day where you didn't feel inspired?

6. Check-in Day:

How are you doing?

What has been working out for you?

What changes have you noticed?

7. Don't expect instant success. You may even become discouraged with how little you see change. Your routine will not always exhibit signs that you are improving. But one day you will compare who you are now, to who you were then, and you will be amazed.

Reflect on a time you gave up on something because it wasn't showing results.

What is one thing you can do daily/weekly that would be life changing in 10 years?

8. The power of a morning routine is life-changing. The first 20 minutes after you wake up will set the stage for the rest of the day. During this time your subconscious mind is most active and you can train your brain to think more positively and accomplish more tasks throughout the day. Devoting this time to something meaningful could quite literally change not only your day, but your entire life.

What can you add to your morning routine to make it more impactful?

What will you need to stop doing in the morning to make sure you have time for what you want to do?

Theme 9:
What Is the Story You're Telling Yourself?

Whatever you tell yourself becomes what you live out. Each of us has a narrative of what we think we are. "I'm bad with money." "I am not a social person." "I do not like sci-fi movies." Are all examples of phrases we tell ourselves that weave together our stories. You are the author, you can write this story however you want. Let's match the stories we tell ourselves with the stories we want to be living. Pick up your pen, because in this theme, we are going to rewrite the story we tell ourselves.

1. The story we tell ourselves has often been told to us by other people.

How have others' opinions of you influenced your own perception of yourself?

What is a positive compliment you have received that motivated you to uphold that trait?

2. We never stop growing, therefore we need to continually challenge our opinions of ourselves.

What is something you could try this week, that you wouldn't normally choose to do?

What is something you learned about yourself from doing something new?

3. Reflection Day:

What are you grateful for today?

What was your favorite part of the day?

What are you looking forward to?

4. The way you speak to yourself has a huge impact on how you perceive yourself.

How do you talk negatively to yourself?

In what ways can you compliment yourself?

5. You are the author. Now bring to life your most authentic story.

Pretend your life is a book or movie.
Write your character description in details:

How can you bring this story to life today?

6. Check-in Day:

How are you doing?

What has been working out for you?

What changes have you noticed?

Theme 10:
Sustainable Habits

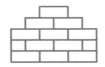

Habits and routines go hand in hand. Your routine should be set up to support your habits and your habits will continue to drive your routine. We often pick up habits from those around us. Living in close quarters in the military, we may have picked up on some not so great habits. Or maybe you had some great habits you would like to get back into. In this theme, we are going to assess your current habits and focus on making new ones sustainable. By making them automatic and easy, they will be an effortless part of your routine.

1. You can't decide your future, but you can decide your habits that will determine your future.

We all know habits can be good or bad. What is a small habit that has changed your life for better or worse?

How do you decide what habit to incorporate in your life?

2. You may have heard of the saying "Tell me who your friends are and I'll tell you who you are." But you could really do the same with habits. Have you ever compared habits with friends or a partner? It is incredible how much habits reveal about a person. A person's habit will show you what they value.

When has someone else's habit inspired you?

What is something you used to do daily, that now you could not see yourself doing?

3. Reflection Day:

What are you grateful for today?

[ ]

What was your favorite part of the day?

[ ]

What are you looking forward to?

[ ]

4. You understand to choose habits that will uphold what you value in life. Now it is time to learn how to make them stick around. When starting something new, it is always great to have a plan and to choose something realistic. Make your new habit an easy and effortless addition to your day. Set up your environment to make your habit a no-brainer. Here are some examples. Want to eat healthier? Shop healthier and keep only nutritious food accessible. Want to reduce screen time? Set screen timers on your phone. (They make it so easy for us now.) Want to run more in the mornings? Set out your running outfit and shoes the night before. Make being impulsive impossible by taking away anything that is tempting.

How is your environment currently setting you up for success?

[ ]

What can you change today to make your habits easier to accomplish?

[ ]

41

5. Sustainable is defined as "able to be maintained at a certain rate or level." Allowing yourself to be able to sustain your habits means it must be a task you can achieve routinely. Think of ways you can enhance your life, not by force, but by increasing the return on something you are already doing.

What is something you do every day that could be elevated by making a minor adjustment? Example: I can not bring my phone to bed, and as a result I spend less time on it.

How have my habits controlled my life in the past?

6. Check-in Day:

How are you doing?

What has been working out for you?

What changes have you noticed?

7. Your habits will grow with you. Sometimes we outgrow habits because we outgrow their value to us. Today I want you to take special notice of everything you do and then ask yourself what the value is behind it. Most of these are going to be obvious, but you may find things that you will question.

Reflect on a time you caught yourself doing something you knew you would regret. How have you learned from this?

What is the value that most recurred throughout your day?

Theme 11:
Setting Your Focus

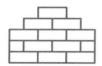

In the military we always had a mission to focus on. Sure, distraction was still around, but it was easier to keep your attention on the target when it was ingrained in everyday life. We may not always have a crucial end goal to keep our sights on, so as a civilian we have to keep ourselves on task. Everything is capable of capturing our attention: thoughts, people, our phones! This is all precious energy that we could be using to make life more beautiful and fulfilling. Remaining focused is a practice that takes patience. Get ready to focus on being focused!

1. Earlier we made clear what our values were. Now we need to stay focused on them. Our time is a precious commodity. Respect your time by staying focused on what you really want to spend your time doing.

How can you honor your attention today?

When has someone taken your time for granted? How did you feel?

2. Being focused is not a one time decision. It is a very active choice that you have to keep making. Sometimes you will even need to make it every couple of seconds or minutes. Think about when you check your phone to only look at the calendar. Next thing you know, you have opened 3 different apps and have completely forgotten the reason you pulled out your phone in the first place. Focus takes practice. Do not become discouraged when you lose it a few times. Keep coming back to your main task.

Think of a task you are going to do soon. How can you make sure you maintain intense focus on this task?

How have you lost focus in the past?

3. Reflection Day:

What are you grateful for today?

What was your favorite part of the day?

What are you looking forward to?

4. When we focus solely on something, we begin to notice more aspects of this task. We can even appreciate the work we are doing through a different perspective.

How have you noticed something new by giving it more attention?

What is in need of your direct focus today?

5. Your reality becomes what you choose to focus on. We do not always focus on things that make us happy. It is human nature to keep looking at the bad. Most times we cannot change the disappointing things around us, but we can shift our focus on what is thriving.

What can you focus on today that will be positive?

What negative things have you given unnecessary attention to lately?

6. Check-in Day:

How are you doing?

What has been working out for you?

What changes have you noticed?

Theme 12:
Creating Your Environment

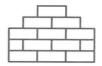

Your environment is defined as the space you are presently in. It is unique to not only you, but to this moment in time as well. The environment around you is constantly changing and is not always in your control. Don't waste time worrying about things in your environment that you cannot change, but contemplate the things you can alter for the better. We are directly impacted by what is around us, so it is important to question what you keep around you and also accept the inevitable aspects of your environment. This theme will explore how we can make our environments work for us.

1. Take a look at everything around you. There may be some things you would like to be different. Maybe you would like some things to be cleaner or less cluttered.

What could you change in your environment today?

What do you have control over in your environment?

2. Life takes us all sorts of interesting places. We can find ourselves in all sorts of situations. Make peace with these places by recognizing yourself as a crucial piece to the environment. You can make each space beautiful.

How can you make peace with your environment this week?

What do you add to your environment just by being present?

3. Reflection Day:

What are you grateful for today?

What was your favorite part of the day?

What are you looking forward to?

4. Make your environment work for you and not against you!

Name something in your current environment that inspires you?

What two things are working for you and what two things are working against you in your environment?

5. An environment that allows growth is important to your development in order to grow. This will mean different things for different people. This may include needing to assess the people, clutter, or noise that fills up your life.

How does your environment allow you to grow?

Reflect on a time where you felt growth was impossible.
How did you overcome it?

6. Check-in Day:

How are you doing?

What has been working out for you?

What changes have you noticed?

7. You are exactly where you need to be. Do not fall into the trap of thinking the next place, job, or partner is going to bring happiness. You are in the perfect environment right now to make it perfectly yours. This excludes dangerous situations. If you are in a safe place, focus on creating your happiness right here and now.

How can you create happiness right here and now?

Reflect on something in your environment that you worked hard to achieve.

Theme 13:
You're Not Missing Out on Anything

Wherever you are in this world right at this moment, is exactly where you are supposed to be. When you get out of the military, you're basically starting over. This can be a time where you compare yourself to what other people your age are doing or what they have. Anchor yourself in the truth that you are exactly where you are meant to be.

1. Sometimes when we think we are missing out, we actually feel like we have been forgotten about. Being away from friends/family while serving, we see everyone continue their lives without us. Even though you are making your own progress, we can feel left behind.

How has your military career made you feel like you have been forgotten about by friends and family?

What was something you were happy you no longer had to deal with, when you left to join the military?

2. "Perception is reality" is a saying you may have heard while serving, and it is the dumbest one because it is so untrue. We keep up with friends and family online, but they are only posting the good stuff. We actually cannot perceive what their reality actually is.

How have you felt bad about yourself while looking at others online?

What brings you peace about exactly where you are right now?

3. Reflection Day:

What are you grateful for today?

What was your favorite part of the day?

What are you looking forward to?

4. With little to no control over certain life circumstances, you may have felt that the military kept you in the same place in life. Or maybe you felt it kept you from living out certain goals. There is no denying the military constrains us in certain ways. No one leaves the military the same as they left, which is proof that there was some growth, lessons learned, or wisdom gained.

Reflect on 2 ways you felt the military kept you from doing something you wanted to. Are you doing them now?

What personal progress do you see in yourself compared to who you were when you joined?

5. When you worry about not doing enough or doing the thing you want, you are taking away from what you are able to do right now.

What are you able to do today that you could completely immerse yourself in?

Write three things you feel you are missing out on now or have missed out on in the past. Then remind yourself that the perfect time will come if it is truly meant to be.

6. Check-in Day:

How are you doing?

What has been working out for you?

What changes have you noticed?

Theme 14:
Un-Numbing

When serving we often become numb to certain parts of our life. This is a coping mechanism that helped us get through a lot of tough times. As we are re-entering society and gaining more control over our lives, we often don't need that tool in our toolbox anymore. However, it's not something you can turn off. You have to actively address and correct it. It may not even be something you have thought of, so let's assess your senses and see where you can become more sensational.

1. Numbing ourselves protects us from the negative emotions, however it also prevents us from feeling the positive ones.

In what ways has your military experience made you numb?
Tell your story, no one is here to judge.

If you feel ready, how could you take a step towards healing in that area of your life?

2. Our unexpressed emotions are stored in our bodies. That is why we often have physical signs of stress/trauma/anxiety. Our body is a direct reflection of our unconscious minds. Connecting with your own body is a great way to release emotions that have been stored up.

How could you connect with your body this week?
Ex: Yoga/self massage/skin care.

In what ways does your body tell you exactly what you need?

3. Reflection Day:

What are you grateful for today?

What was your favorite part of the day?

What are you looking forward to?

4. Expressing yourself through creativity does wonders for reconnecting with your senses. For example: working with our hands to make something physical or working with our brains to write something. When we connect our bodies with what we are feeling through art, it's like magic.

In what way do you consider yourself creative?

What is your favorite way to express yourself?

5. Our numbness may have started before the military. You may have already experienced childhood trauma that you carried with you into the service. That trauma was then exacerbated by serving. We all carry that vulnerable inner child within us. If you are having a hard time with self-compassion, think of a younger version of yourself.

What would you say to your younger self if they felt they couldn't express their pain?

How does thinking of your younger self motivate you to keep working on your present self?

6. Check-in Day:

How are you doing?

What has been working out for you?

What changes have you noticed?

7. Contrary to numbness, we do have those rare moments of feeling fully alive. Everything seems amplified. Sounds are clearer, food tastes better, and everything feels more vibrant.

Reflect on a time where you felt fully alive. Describe all 5 senses in that moment.

What or who makes you feel fully alive?

Theme 15:
Mindfulness

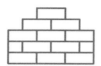

Mindfulness can sound a little "woo woo" however it is a really practical practice. It is acknowledging the world around you in an intentional way. The benefits of thinking like this actually promotes positive changes in your brain. If this is your first time, come in with zero expectations. Like any skill, it takes practice. During this theme you will have a challenge each day along with your journal entries.

1. Treat each task as if it is the only thing you are doing that day. Give it your full undivided attention and see how much quicker you will get things done.

How can you be more in the moment while doing everyday tasks?

What in your life do you wish you paid more attention to and why?

2. Take notice of your thoughts. Question them. Ponder where they may come from and how they make you feel.

Write down any negative thoughts you have had in the past week. Where do you think they come from?

What reminders can you set up throughout your day to be kinder to yourself?

3. Reflection Day:

What are you grateful for today?

[   ]

What was your favorite part of the day?

[   ]

What are you looking forward to?

[   ]

4. Be mindful of your body. Take note of the wonder you walk around in every day.

What can you thank your body for today?

[   ]

How can being more mindful of your body lead to healthier decisions?

[   ]

5. So often our attention is either all over the place or so jet-focused on something that we don't even notice what our senses are experiencing. Choose one moment today to fully take in all five senses. Become aware of what you see, hear, feel, touch, and taste.

How can being fully present help you to worry less?

When your mind wonders, what helps you bring it back to center?

6. Check-in Day:

How are you doing?

What has been working out for you?

What changes have you noticed?

Theme 16:
What Your Service Means to You

Our service can mean something different to us after we get out compared to when we first joined. We have gained new information on what the military is actually like and we learned more about our military's role in the world as a whole. As veterans, we may be questioned on our perspective of the military or current events involving the military. You don't have any responsibility to respond, however such questions can bring up mixed feelings. During this theme you are going to reflect on what your service means/meant to you.

1. We all had a reason behind our decision for joining. Every decision involved a vision of a better future.

What were a few of the reasons you joined the military?

How did you picture what your life would be like while in the military?

2. We all had a picture in our heads of what the military did or what role it played in our global society. But you can't fully understand it until you are a part of it.

How did you think your position in the military would help the world at large?

What impacts did you witness the military make either on a global or local scale?

3. Reflection Day:

What are you grateful for today?

What was your favorite part of the day?

What are you looking forward to?

4. Working for the government opens you up to a whole new perspective of how our country really works.

How do you view our country differently after serving?

In what ways has serving made you more grateful to be an American? Less grateful?

5. When in uniform, society can look at us as "heroes." We are given a lot of positive attention while serving and feel a sense of pride in our jobs/role. When getting out, we may not feel that pride in our current job.

In what ways did you find pride in serving in the military?

How can you find pride in your current role?

6. Check-in Day:

How are you doing?

What has been working out for you?

What changes have you noticed?

Theme 17:
Community

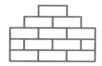

You may miss the sense of community that the military brought you. Even though it didn't always feel like it, you did have a support system while serving. While wearing the same uniform as others, you also had a firm sense of belonging. After getting out you may move somewhere new and not have that sense of community anymore. Having people around you that have your well-being in mind is so important, but it's not always attainable for veterans. In this theme, we are going to look into your options for communal support and define your support system.

1. As humans we have a deep need for connection. We are social creatures and psychologically crave meaningful connections with others.

What sense of a community do you currently have?

How can you meet your need for connection?

2. Having a support system improves both physical and mental health. This looks different for everyone. Some people need a huge support system, while others may depend on one or two people. It takes time, but you can build your support system by taking a chance to trust others. It is also constantly changing and you have the power in deciding who gets to be a part of it or not.

Identify who is in your support system.
Who could you work on adding to this list?

How has your support system changed throughout your life?

3. Reflection Day:

What are you grateful for today?

What was your favorite part of the day?

What are you looking forward to?

4. The best way to gain community is to put yourself out there. This is uncomfortable at first, but it will pay off. Just by being a veteran you already have several opportunities to be a part of a community.

How can you put yourself out there this week to be more involved, or to start getting involved in a community you respect?

You have so much to offer. Make a list of what you bring to the table when meeting in community.

5. With the internet we can find community at our fingertips. Although people online won't be in your proximity, they can provide a sense of camaraderie and share beneficial information. An internet bond can be a fine line to toe, but it has the power to make us feel less alone.

What online communities are you a part of? Which ones would you consider being a part of?

How has the internet connected you with others?

6. Check-in Day:

How are you doing?

What has been working out for you?

What changes have you noticed?

Theme 18:
Continuing to Serve

Serving in the military may not have always felt like a service to others, but it absolutely was. Most of your days were spent doing something for others. However, that doesn't mean you didn't gain personally from this. Some of our best self discovery is found while putting others' needs above ours. When you get out, you may not view your day to day jobs as having a higher purpose, but looking closer you will see that there most definitely is. This theme will dive into how to rediscover yourself, by your service to those around you.

1. "The best way to find yourself is to lose yourself in the service of others" - Gandhi

What is one way that you have served others that has stuck with you?

What did you learn about yourself while serving someone else?

2. Serving others does not look like people pleasing or being taken advantage of. Service is something that is done out of love. Trying to please everyone or letting others take advantage of you is done out of fear.

How have you let others take advantage of you in the past?

When have you avoided an opportunity to serve others due to the fear of being taken advantage of?

3. Reflection Day:

What are you grateful for today?

What was your favorite part of the day?

What are you looking forward to?

4. Service has nothing to do with the person you are serving and everything to do with the person you are becoming.

How have you questioned if someone was worthy enough to receive your act of kindness?

When you serve others, what is your deepest intention behind it?

5. We do not exist in vacuums. You serve and are served by other people everyday whether you directly see it or not.

How does your current role help others in their lives?

In what ways is your community of service to you?

6. Check-in Day:

How are you doing?

What has been working out for you?

What changes have you noticed?

Theme 19:
Health

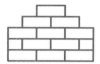

Our health is our #1 investment. Even though it is so significant to our well-being, we can sometimes put it on the back burner. In the military we were encouraged to take care of our health, but we were also given limited options on what that could look like. Working in a fast-paced environment often had us relying on unhealthy coping mechanisms. Also, going to medical was mostly at the mercy of our superiors. During this theme, we are going to reflect on your relationship with your own health and see how it can be improved.

1. We don't often take a second to truly assess our current state of health, here's your opportunity. Start from your head all the way down to your toes.

What about your physical or mental health is concerning you right now?

If you could wave a magic wand and fix your health problems, how would you address these concerns?

2. Let's talk about health care. In the military you were fully covered and that may not be the case anymore. You are now in charge of how your health care needs are being taken care of.

How would you handle a major medical emergency if it happened today? Think both financially, resourcefully, and mentally.

How can you make sure all of your healthcare needs will be met when needed?

3. Reflection Day:

What are you grateful for today?

[ ]

What was your favorite part of the day?

[ ]

What are you looking forward to?

[ ]

4. Health is a very personal thing. There is no right or wrong way to approach your health and everyone does so differently.

How has your relationship with your health been in the past?

[ ]

How has your family impacted your health approaches?

[ ]

How has the military impacted the way you take care of yourself?

[ ]

5. The military's main focus on health mostly has to do with fitness and nutrition. However, health is more complex than that. Here are some aspects of health that can often be overlooked: emotional, social, spiritual, and environmental.

What aspect of your health do you pay the least attention to?

What aspect of your health needs the most attention and why?

6. Check-in Day:

How are you doing?

What has been working out for you?

What changes have you noticed?

Theme 20:
Trust Yourself

"Trust your gut. Always trust your gut. More than the words of others. More than the actions of others. Trust yourself enough to know that you have instincts for a reason and that those instincts should be trusted."
- Unknown

You have not gotten yourself here by pure chance. Your intuition has directed you through every choice. After serving in the military, trust within yourself may need some rebuilding. When working in high stress environments, your trust moves from trusting yourself to trusting others. This is essential for working in those conditions, however you are not in that place anymore. During this theme, we are going to focus on how you can lean into your intuition and trust yourself deeper.

1. Your subconscious mind can pick up on cues that you don't even realize are happening. We have feelings about things before we understand them because our body knows before our conscious mind does.

When and how has your body told you that something was off but you couldn't figure out what it was until later?

In what ways does your body let you know that something isn't right?

2. Intuition and being paranoid are two different things that can be confused. Intuition allows you to understand something without conscious reasoning, whereas paranoia stems from fear and is often exaggerated or unjustified.

What is something that has made you paranoid in the past?

What is the most recent unjustified worry you have had that may have seemed unreasonable? Decide if this is intuition or paranoia.

3. Reflection Day:

What are you grateful for today?

What was your favorite part of the day?

What are you looking forward to?

4. You know yourself best, but sometimes it is hard to give ourselves undivided attention. In order to trust our intuition we need to check in with ourselves so we can listen.

How do you currently check in with your body? If you don't, how can you do so today?

In what part of your life do you want to trust yourself more?

5. The brain and the gastrointestinal system are intimately connected. Therefore your gut feeling is a real signal to your brain. The more you understand it, the more you can trust it.

When has a gut feeling led you in the right direction?

What do you feel like you currently trust the most out of the following: your brain, your heart, or your gut? Why?

6. Check-in Day:

How are you doing?

What has been working out for you?

What changes have you noticed?

Theme 21:
Stress

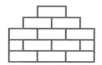

Stress was without a doubt a daily occurrence in the military. Defined as "a state of worry or mental tension caused by a difficult situation," we all know what stress is and how it feels. It can show up in all sorts of ways; through our actions, in our physical body, and definitely in our thoughts. How each of us copes with stress is unique and personal. During this theme, we are going to reflect on how you deal with stress.

1. Stress isn't caused by what is going on in your life, but by your thoughts about what's going on in your life.

What does your internal dialogue sound like when you are going through something stressful?

How can you control your thoughts when you can't control your situation?

2. When we feel stressed, we just want some relief. This can sometimes lead to impulsive or reckless decisions. By setting up healthy responses to stress, we can prevent ourselves from regretting those instant reactions to stress.

What is your go-to coping mechanism when you feel stressed out?

List three things that help you relieve stress in a healthy way:

3. Reflection Day:

What are you grateful for today?

What was your favorite part of the day?

What are you looking forward to?

4. Our stresses are often something that occur regularly. By identifying these daily or weekly stressors we can find a way to make them less impactful.

What is the most stressful part of your day?

How could you prepare yourself to make a stressful part of your day a little easier?

5. Navigating the world after service is not an easy thing. No matter how long it has been, you may just feel overwhelmed with life in general. That is totally okay, and normal! Stress is going to happen and stressing about stress only leads to (you guessed it) more stress.

What has been your biggest stressor since separating from the military?

Compare your stress levels from when you were in the military to your current point in life. What has changed?

6. Check-in Day:

How are you doing?

What has been working out for you?

What changes have you noticed?

Theme 22:
Confidence

It's not something you are born with or something that has a secret formula. In its simplest definition, confidence is "the willingness to try." This is grounded in self-trust. It isn't the trust that you know you can do something, but the trust that you will be okay no matter what the results are. After the military, our self-assurance can be put into question. During these next entries, we are going to see where your confidence is at how it can become more consistent.

1. Confidence is not fixed. It will change in different scenarios, around different people, and in new situations. But no matter where you happen to be, you can always have confidence in yourself.

In what situations do you feel most confident? Why may that be?

Reflect on a time your confidence was boosted and how that came to be.

2. Confidence doesn't come from always being right, but from not fearing to be wrong.

When was the last time you did something that scared the shit out of you?

How have you handled being wrong in the past?

3. Reflection Day:

What are you grateful for today?

What was your favorite part of the day?

What are you looking forward to?

4. Build confidence through trust. Accept yourself just as you are in this moment. The perfect imperfection that you are. You know yourself more than anyone and because you understand yourself, you can trust yourself.

What is a promise you have made to yourself that you have kept?

Describe something about yourself you can work to fully accept.

5. Confidence can grow by attempting new things. Remember, it isn't about succeeding at something new, it's simply putting yourself out there.

What is something new you want to try?

How can you put yourself slightly outside your comfort zone today?

6. Check-in Day:

How are you doing?

What has been working out for you?

What changes have you noticed?

Theme 23:
What Is Success?

You may feel pressure to be successful after service. When we announce we are getting out, others may doubt your decision. Some may have even said you won't be successful without the military. Success is something we are told we all should strive to achieve. There are many ways we can be viewed as successful by society, but is that what we really want? Success has to be personally defined in order for it to be authentic. Measuring it on any other terms will not be satisfying. In this theme, we are going to define what success means to you.

1. Our view of success is often shaped by our past as well as those around us.

What is an example of what your family/friends would deem successful?

Who is someone you view as successful and why?

2. Success has nothing to do with skill, effort, or accomplishments and everything to do with perspective.

How can you view your present self as successful?

What would you have to accomplish for you to view yourself as successful?

3. Reflection Day:

What are you grateful for today?

[ ]

What was your favorite part of the day?

[ ]

What are you looking forward to?

[ ]

4. Success is something we can achieve every day by counting the little wins.

What is the smallest thing you accomplished today?

[ ]

In what area of your life do you find success comes easily?

[ ]

5. Don't compare others' success with your own. (1) You probably aren't trying to obtain the same goals as them (2) You didn't start out with the same background, resources, or opportunities.

Who or what have you been comparing yourself with?

Compare yourself with yourself from 5 years ago. How have you grown?

6. Check-in Day:

How are you doing?

What has been working out for you?

What changes have you noticed?

Theme 24:
Excuses

Excuses are like assholes, we all have them and they all stink. Think about it, you can come up with an excuse for everything. They are as real as you want them to be. So during this theme we are going to dismiss our excuses and make a deal to never use them again.

1. Know the difference between an excuse and an explanation. An explanation is based on real circumstances. An excuse is based on feelings and can be made up.

What are some excuses you currently use as explanations?

When have you leaned on an excuse to keep yourself comfortable?

2. If you are going after something you want, excuses will not work.

What is an excuse you have ignored while pushing towards something you wanted to achieve or have?

How has someone used an excuse that ended up hurting your relationship?

3. Reflection Day:

What are you grateful for today?

What was your favorite part of the day?

What are you looking forward to?

4. Excuses will always be there for you, opportunities won't.

How has an excuse gotten in the way of an opportunity?

How have you used an excuse to get out of something you didn't want to do?

5. Excuses are lies you tell yourself. What are your current excuses?

Let's dissect these excuses in the chart below.

Task you need to do	What you are telling yourself (excuse)	What is really happening (reality)	Solution

Some excuses can be pretty outrageous. What is the funniest excuse you have ever heard or used?

6. Check-in Day:

How are you doing?

What has been working out for you?

What changes have you noticed?

101

Theme 25:
Hack Your Brain

Our brain is the most complex part of the human body, but that doesn't mean it can't be tricked! The mind and body are undoubtedly connected. We can purposely hold our bodies in ways that give the mind an impression of something that it wouldn't otherwise feel. Let's try a few challenges through this theme and see how they work out for you.

1. In boot camp, a smile could have gotten you into a world of trouble. But today you can consider it a tool. Whether it's real or not, smiling directly stimulates the feeling of wellbeing in the brain. Create a smile at 3 random points today. Bonus: make one in the mirror.

Where/when were you able to fit in those smiles today?

How did it break up an otherwise insignificant moment?

Why does it feel so awkward to smile at yourself in the mirror?

2. Good posture is a signature lesson in boot camp. But standing at attention gives us more than just discipline, it actually increases testosterone and decreases cortisol. Put a little extra effort into your posture today. Whether it's while brushing your teeth or in the car, put your shoulders back and hold your head a little higher.

How do you feel when you have good posture?

What parts of your day do you wish you had better posture?

3. Reflection Day:

What are you grateful for today?

What was your favorite part of the day?

What are you looking forward to?

4. This one is going to seem extra corny, however it is pretty powerful. We can get comfort from others through physical affection, but you can also get it from yourself. Hugging yourself may seem unnatural, but it is pretty beneficial! A hug from yourself has been proven to relieve pain, help you feel safe, improve mood, and increase self-compassion.

Give yourself the type of hug you need at this moment.
How did that make you feel?

What did you think about while you were hugging yourself?

5. We hold so much tension in our bodies. The normal places we think of being tense are our shoulders, back, or neck. However, neuroscience indicates our hips are a storage vessel for our emotions. Stretching or putting extra care into our hips could help our bodies release trauma.

Have you ever felt tension in your hips? What may have been the cause of that tension?

What part of your body do you feel most tense?

6. Check-in Day:

How are you doing?

What has been working out for you?

What changes have you noticed?

Theme 26:
What Is Happiness?

Happiness is often mistaken for temporary pleasure. It is not a destination or something you can buy. You aren't going to find it in another person. It isn't automatic, it is a conscious realization. That is the most beautiful part, it is something we can create. It comes from within ourselves, but our brains aren't programmed to look for it. Our ancient brains are designed to look for danger. We need to consciously remind our brains to realize the happiness in our world. Happiness isn't fixed. We aren't allotted a certain amount, and once used up it's gone forever. It's unlimited!

1. For something to truly bring you happiness, it must not bring you guilt later.

Reflect on a time where you have mistaken temporary pleasure for happiness.

How do you currently decipher between pleasure and happiness?

2. No matter what your situation or status, we are all in pursuit of happiness. This means that happiness actually has nothing to do with other people or what we have. Happiness starts from within ourselves.

In what ways do you feel at peace with yourself?

Describe 5 things you appreciate about yourself.

3. Reflection Day:

What are you grateful for today?

What was your favorite part of the day?

What are you looking forward to?

4. If you aren't sure what happiness is, let's decide what it is not.

What is something you thought would bring you happiness but ultimately didn't?

What is your guilty pleasure and where did it start?

5. One way to ensure happiness is by setting yourself up so happiness is automatic.

How could you add daily reminders of happiness in your life?

Now for the big one: what makes you truly happy?

6. Check-in Day:

How are you doing?

What has been working out for you?

What changes have you noticed?

Theme 27:
Efficiently Efficient

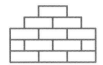

Being efficient was often rewarded in the military. With limited resources and high demand, we often had to make the most with the least. There wasn't time or place for extra baggage to be brought along. We learned how to cut out all of the unnecessary to make room for the essential. Tapping into that mindset, get ready to trim everything unnecessary from your life. Throughout your day, the things you choose not to do are just as important as the things you choose to do. Start small. With everything you are giving energy towards, you are taking it away from somewhere.

1. You can't increase the habits you want without decreasing the ones you don't.

What unnecessary habits can you remove from your day?

How do you feel today?

2. The more you let go, the higher you rise

What can you let go of today?

Where is your happy place?

3. Reflection Day:

What are you grateful for today?

What was your favorite part of the day?

What are you looking forward to?

4. We can add value by taking away, however do not plan to do it all at once. "The man who removes a mountain begins by carrying away small stones." - Chinese Proverbs

What is a distraction you want to be rid of?

What is something that causes you to waste time?

5. Cutting out negative thinking, makes a place for positive thoughts.

How often do you catch yourself thinking negatively?

What is a positive thing that happened to you today?

6. Check-in Day:

How are you doing?

What has been working out for you?

What changes have you noticed?

Theme 28:
Defeating Self-Sabotage Campaigns

We can often be our own worst enemy. A lot of times this happens because deep down we don't feel deserving. This stems from fear. We feel we aren't worthy of love, happiness, friendship, career, etc. So we tend to sabotage ourselves, before something else has the chance to ruin things for us. No matter what you have been through or what type of person you are, you deserve to move on and elevate your life. Let's define your self-sabotage campaign and create our own smear campaign against it.

1. Becoming aware of how you root against yourself is the first step. You may not even realize you do this, but it can be as simple as procrastination or under-preparing for something.

How have you kept yourself from achieving something you wanted?

What are a few of your biggest distractors right now?

2. Treat yourself with compassion when you find yourself avoiding a task you know you should be doing. Often we create more guilt by not doing what we wanted to do, and end up doing even less.

When you feel like you aren't doing what you are supposed to be doing, how do you react?

Pretend you are an outsider looking in, what advice would you give yourself when you are self-sabotaging?

3. Reflection Day:

What are you grateful for today?

What was your favorite part of the day?

What are you looking forward to?

4. You won't wake up one day and be completely free of your negative behaviors. However, they can slowly become less tempting.

What motivates you to focus on what you truly want out of life?

How can you make negative behaviors less tempting?

5. By picking up this workbook, you have already decided that you are worthy of putting effort into yourself. I am proud of you!

What is something you've accomplished and you look back on with pride?

Create a saying that will remind you that you are worthy.

6. Check-in Day:

How are you doing?

What has been working out for you?

What changes have you noticed?

Theme 29:
Patience Is Not Passive

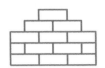

Hurry up and wait was a phrase used often in the military. However frustrating, it helped us practice patience. We had to be prepared because we never knew when the perfect timing would happen. Being patient is trusting the process in whatever you are doing. Currently you are trying to make the best from your transition out of the military. You are making small adjustments here and there to better your quality of life. Most of the changes you make are not going to be noticeable for a while. Having patience and knowing that every good choice you make counts, will help keep your spirit up. During this theme, try to practice being patient with yourself, others, and the world around you.

1. Patience is so much more than being good at waiting. It is a choice we have to actively make. Think about meditation, when you get distracted you have to return your mind to calm. This may happen several times during a session. Patience falls under the same concept. When we start to doubt our practices or values, we need to return to patience.

Write down some of your most common worries/fears.

How could practicing patience help ease these anxieties?

2. Patience is a type of wisdom. It shows us that we understand the fact that things must unfold in their own time.

Reflect on a time when you wanted something to happen, and now looking back, you are so glad it didn't.

How has your relationship with patience been in the past?

3. Reflection Day:

What are you grateful for today?

What was your favorite part of the day?

What are you looking forward to?

4. You are not an overnight success. You are a work in progress who has no limit on how far they will go. Each day you are putting in the work to become better and understand yourself on deeper levels than you have ever thought possible. Do not question your progression. Stand firm in your patience. You are worth it!

How can you give yourself more patience this week?

Reflect on a time when someone was patient with you. How did that affect you?

5. The secret of patience is to keep yourself occupied in the meantime.

What are ways you tend to occupy yourself while waiting for something else to happen?

6. Check-in Day:

How are you doing?

What has been working out for you?

What changes have you noticed?

7. Patience is a great way to honor the time we have. Our time is limited and society makes us feel the need to hit benchmarks at certain points in our life. There is no timeline for happiness. Be patient with your life, and accept you are exactly where you are supposed to be.

When have you felt the pressure of society's expectations?

Reflect on something others may view "out of order."
How has that benefited you in the end?

Theme 30:
You Are Gratitude

In any rough work environment, complaining is contagious. Unfortunately the military is no exception. It is relatable to complain about things and can seem socially acceptable, however focusing on the negativity can wear on you after a while. Gratitude is focusing on the positive. Being truly gracious for something comes from being absolutely present in a moment and giving an object, person, or experience true honor. It takes practice, but we can train our minds to react with gratitude. We can find a way to be grateful for anything, so let's get to practicing.

1. Make gratitude your default setting and watch your life change. Try to start and end each day by thinking of a few things you are grateful for. Over time this will become an automatic response and change your thought process to focus on the positive.

Name four things you are grateful for right now:

What has your relationship with gratitude been like in the past?

2. We all have facts about our past that we are not the most proud of. But you would not be where you are today if it weren't for these events. Give your past self grace and let go of any hold your past has on you. Be grateful for how far you have come and where you are going.

How can you give your past self grace?

What is an event in your past that made you who you are today?

3. Reflection Day:

What are you grateful for today?

What was your favorite part of the day?

What are you looking forward to?

4. Gratitude helps you focus on what is right there in front of you. It centers you in your present moment and helps you to notice all of the beautiful things you already have in your life. By practicing gratitude, we can recognize that most of our "needs" are actually "wants." We have an abundance of so many wonderful things right at our disposal.

What are 3 things you have an abundance of right now?

What will you take notice of today that yesterday you may have taken for granted?

5. Gratitude is contagious! It is not something to keep to ourselves and is actually more gratifying to share. Tell others what you are thankful for and do it often. If you live with another person(s), start to say out loud how much you appreciate everyday occurrences. Watch the atmosphere change!

How will you communicate your gratitude today?

Reflect on a time when someone was grateful for something that you saw as insignificant.

6. Check-in Day:

How are you doing?

What has been working out for you?

What changes have you noticed?

7. In this theme we learned how to fall in love with the life you already have. Of course there are things we want to work on or change, but how beautiful is it to have those opportunities!

How will you continue your journey of falling in love with your life?

What is an opportunity of growth you currently have?

Theme 31:
Setting Your Intentions

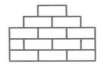

Intentions are simply what you intend to do. This can be for the day, the year, or your life. Intentions come from the core of your heart. Intentions are carried inside us and it is important to remember that other people are unaware of them. By living out our intentions we are sharing them with the world. This theme will help you identify what your intentions are and how you can use them to be your most authentic self.

1. Intentions aren't as detailed as goals. There is a lot of wiggle room as to what you intend to do. Use this creatively and try to think in the abstract when deciding your current intentions.

What personal actions would make your life better?

How could you live your life so it enables you to give and receive more love?

2. A helpful way to create or discover your intentions is to think about how you navigate through everyday life.

What do you want to prioritize?

What do you want to consume (food/media)?

3. Reflection Day:

What are you grateful for today?

What was your favorite part of the day?

What are you looking forward to?

4. Today is going to be incredible. Why? Because you just decided it right now! Today is going to come and go before you know it. You have already devoted yourself to this day by opening this workbook, you are amazing!

What was something you did that brought your life enrichment?

What is a pastime you enjoy that makes you feel fulfilled?

5. By frequently reminding ourselves of our intentions we are signaling our unconscious mind to look for them in everyday life.

How can you consciously remind yourself of your intentions?

Think of intentions you've had in the past, how have they changed?

6. Check-in Day:

How are you doing?

What has been working out for you?

What changes have you noticed?

Theme 32:
Challenge Yourself

    Challenges are all around us and they don't have to be a huge feat to be rewarding. You are already challenging yourself by doing this workbook. We were constantly challenged in the military, often with tasks we didn't want to do in the first place. Despite the context of the challenge, it is always an opportunity for growth. Challenging yourself is a great way to find purpose and to grow as a person. This theme we are going to re-think challenges from being intimidating to something you will look forward to.

1. Let's start small. Creating a new challenge does not have to be an elaborate design. A challenge is anything that puts you outside your comfort zone. Tailor these challenges to something you want to work on. Maybe you have been isolated and need to reconnect? Challenge yourself to text an old friend once this week. Or perhaps you want to drink more water? Challenge yourself to finish a glass of water before you eat breakfast or have your morning coffee.

What is a small area in your life you would like to work on?

How can you create a challenge from this?

2. Re-framing a problem or an issue as a challenge, is a great way to change your perspective on it. The way we think about adversities in our life will change the way we approach them. By telling yourself this is a challenge instead of a problem, you may have less anxiety around the issue.

How can you re-define a current problem as a challenge?

How have you dealt with problems in the past?

3. Reflection Day:

What are you grateful for today?

[ ]

What was your favorite part of the day?

[ ]

What are you looking forward to?

[ ]

4. Whether you are having a challenging day or maybe are in the middle of a new challenge at work, it is important to have the right mindset. Remind yourself why you are doing this and motivate yourself to keep moving past roadblocks. Also remind yourself it is always okay to ask for help.

What is something you have to do today, that you can give a new perspective to?

[ ]

How can you remind yourself that although the challenge is tough, you are learning every time?

[ ]

5. Sometimes life challenges us with some pretty shitty situations. A great tool to use when in the middle of a problem, is to remind yourself that it is temporary. This challenge will pass and you will become better because of it.

What is something challenging you that you know will be rewarding?

Write a few reasons your current challenges are worth it.

6. Check-in Day:

How are you doing?

What has been working out for you?

What changes have you noticed?

Theme 33:
Breathing Big

There are moments in life where we just need to take a deep breath and step back. Think of this theme as one big breath preparing you to let it all out. To breathe deep we need to create space in ourselves by opening both our souls and our minds. Breathing is a constant in our lives, therefore we should give it the attention it deserves.

1. Life happens in the blink of an eye. Before we know it, we are going to be wondering, "where did all the time go?" These days full of hustle and bustle never seem to let up. Sometimes we need to slow down or even downshift when life seems like it is going way too fast.

How can you slow down time this week?

What has been consuming most of your time lately?

2. The beautiful thing about breathing is we don't ever have to think about it, it's automatic. When we are intentional about breathing it can transform us. Those moments when you take a deep breath or meditate on the inhales and exhales ground you to the natural phenomena of your body.

Name two times during the day you could use a deep breath

How has your body been feeling?

3. Reflection Day:

What are you grateful for today?

What was your favorite part of the day?

What are you looking forward to?

4. Inhale for 5 seconds, hold for 5 seconds, exhale for 5 seconds and repeat. Our lungs have so much more room than we usually use. When you use your lung's full capacity you can feel the difference.

Think of other spaces in your life that aren't fully used up. Could you improve your life by making use of them?

Where else in your life can you use your body's full potential?

5. When we are going through something difficult, breathing can go on the backburner. However, breathing is the one thing that could get us through it! That is why breathing in labor is always emphasized as the main focus. It can ease our pain and put our biological needs in front, where they belong.

Have you ever been focusing on something so hard that you almost forgot to breathe? If so, explain.

What types of difficult situations may arise in the future that breathing can help you with?

6. Check-in Day:

How are you doing?

What has been working out for you?

What changes have you noticed?

7. Breathing is inviting new life into your body. Each breath takes what you need and exhales what you don't. Breathing is like saying yes to the beautiful things life has to offer and exhaling is saying no to the things that aren't necessary.

How can you say yes to more beautiful things?

How can you say no to more unnecessary things?

Theme 34:
Beware of Destination Addiction

Destination addiction is the cycle of searching for happiness in a desired goal. This goal can be a new house, new job, new partner, or anything you have been wanting. We bank on these goals to make our dreams come true and often neglect everything else until that goal is achieved. Once the goal is reached and the happiness we were hoping for isnt there, it can leave us feeling empty. The solution is often to find another goal to achieve, hoping there will be happiness there.

1. Deciding that all the joy is at the next destination in life, takes away from the joy in this present moment. You may look back on today and view it as a "simpler" time.

What is something you worked for that you thought would bring happiness?

Picture yourself in five years. How do you think you would look back at this present part of your life?

2. Achieving something new is very rewarding. Working hard towards something gives us satisfaction and reminds us that we can do great things. Working towards something is also exciting. It gives you a task to do every day and know that it will be worth it. This mindset is not to be confused with that of destination addiction, in which you feel you will not be happy until you are at the desired place. Here is an example statement. "Once I graduate and get my dream job, then I will finally be happy."

How do you enjoy the ins and outs of your day-to-day striving towards a goal?

Reflect on a time when the journey was just as pleasurable as the destination.

3. Reflection Day:

What are you grateful for today?

What was your favorite part of the day?

What are you looking forward to?

4. You are working everyday to become a better version of yourself. Embrace every struggle and cherish every hardship. Remember: this active choice to be better is a lifestyle, not a destination.

How can you make an unpleasant task fun today?

What has been your biggest accomplishment in the past year?

5. "The grass isn't always greener on the other side." We have all heard this cliché quote a million times, however it packs a great point! It doesn't matter what is on the other side, learn to appreciate your own grass.

Give me two details that are amazing about your life right now.

How have you been jealous of others in the past, only to realize their grass wasn't greener?

6. Check-in Day:

How are you doing?

What has been working out for you?

What changes have you noticed?

7. "The foolish man seeks happiness in the distance, the wise grows it under his feet". -James Oppenheim

How are you growing happiness under your feet?

Where have you sought happiness in the past?

Theme 35:
Power of Perseverance

Perseverance is "persistence in doing something, despite difficulty or delay in achieving success." It is the tool that you will need to utilize every time you feel like giving up on something you know you want to achieve.

1. Perseverance is a series of short sprints, not just one long marathon.

What is a "short sprint" you have recently finished?

How have you gotten through hard times in the past?

2. Whether it is consciously or not, you choose to work towards something every day. The level of effort won't always be the same, but you are still moving forward. Perseverance is happening without us even knowing. Now imagine if you put more intention behind that forward motion. You may move a little faster.

What daily task could you put more intention behind?

How have you been moving forward?

3. Reflection Day:

What are you grateful for today?

What was your favorite part of the day?

What are you looking forward to?

4. Sometimes we see how long something will take and decide it is not worth it. Many times this thinking is practical, however, time is going to pass regardless of what you do.

How has a time commitment deterred you from an opportunity in the past?

Reflect on a recent decision you are thankful for.

5. When working towards a goal or habit, you will find times when you have to walk away. This could be due to life events, new schedules, etc. Taking a break is sometimes a good thing, as long as you come back to it. That is perseverance!

When have you had to take a break in the past?

What was the most enjoyable part of your week so far?

6. Check-in Day:

How are you doing?

What has been working out for you?

What changes have you noticed?

7. The most important part of perseverance is knowing your energy is going in the right direction. Being consistent and persistent isn't enough. You need to check in from time to time to know that your efforts are worth it. A casual check in can help you gauge where you are at in your progress and it can also re-inspire you as to why you have started something in the first place.

How can you reevaluate your current efforts toward a goal?

Reflect on a time your perseverance paid off.

Theme 36:
Debunking Personal Truths

In this theme, you are going to think about everything you ever thought was true about yourself. Any fact or narrative you have about yourself is now going to be in question. These truths can be very core to who you believe you are as a person. Often times, these personal truths can be negative. Here are some examples: "I'm not a math person," "Running is not my thing," or "I've never been good at reading." Many of these truths we carry with us, aren't actually true at all. Sometimes they were assigned to us by others or we decided them at a very young age. But that doesn't mean they get to define who we are now. Let's get into them and find out the root cause of these beliefs.

1. Personal truths are anything we believe to be consistent about ourselves. They are used to guide us through life and are a way we rationalize our decisions. Some of these truths have been with us since we were young. It is important to identify and assess these truths often because they may be outdated.

List three negative personal truths you have:

Discuss the proof you have to justify each of these truths.

2. Sometimes personal truths are convenient to us because we use them as excuses. These self-beliefs may be our justification as to why we continue some habits or avoid change.

When, in the past, have you used a personal truth as an excuse?

How have others used personal truths as excuses around you?

3. Reflection Day:

What are you grateful for today?

What was your favorite part of the day?

What are you looking forward to?

4. Our personal truths often come from the minds of others.

Think about teachers, parents, or other influences in your life. Who has defined a personal truth for you?

How have you changed the narrative around your personal truths?

5. Let go of any narrative that tells you who you are supposed to be.

Reflect on an opportunity you passed on because you thought it was not the right fit.

How can you empower yourself with a new personal truth?

6. Check-in Day:

How are you doing?

What has been working out for you?

What changes have you noticed?

154

7. Our personal truths have navigated us through life thus far. We may have used them to decide the type of partner we want, to define our sense of humor, or how we present our physical self to the world. We can't always pinpoint the moment our personal truths change, but we can review them and make sure they are still important to us.

What personal truths did this workbook help you question?

What is a funny personal truth you used to believe?

Theme 37:
The Medicine Called Laughter

Laughter is what got us through a lot of hard times in the military. We didn't have much control over our circumstances, but we could always feel better with a good laugh. Let's lean into that humor and do something that makes you laugh.

1. Whether it's a funny movie, a stand up comedian, or telling an inside joke with a friend. Laughter makes us feel good. It's a gentle reminder that we don't have to be so serious.

Laughter releases endorphins and even increases our thresholds for pain. How have you used laughter to get you through a painful time?

When was the last time you had a really good laugh?

2. The military gives you a sense of humor like no other. More humor means more happiness and less stress. But does dark humor count? If so, we are golden.

What is something or someone that always makes you laugh?

Learn one new joke and write it below.

3. Reflection Day:

What are you grateful for today?

What was your favorite part of the day?

What are you looking forward to?

4. Statistics show that once you hit twenty-three, you start to laugh a lot less often. Four year olds laugh 300 times a day, while at forty, it takes you two months to laugh that much

In what situations do you notice you laugh more often?

Why do you think people stop laughing as much when they get older?

5. Humor is a great way to be human. It is a powerful way to relate and connect with others.

Has humor ever connected you with someone or something unexpected?

Recall a time when a comedic relief really saved the day

6. Check-in Day:

How are you doing?

What has been working out for you?

What changes have you noticed?

Theme 38:
What Really Matters?

During this theme, we are going to tie in several of our past journal entries and decide what is truly important to you. We all get caught up in the politics or dramas of life. Peel those distractions back and look at the core of what matters to you. By finding out what you actually care about, you can focus less on all of life's distractions.

1. A lot of what we currently care about may be influenced by societal pressure. Can you imagine how different you would be if you didn't conform to what society wants you to be? Maybe you are more of a rebel and don't think you are influenced, however there is no way to fully be free of these standards. Societal norms and pressures are constantly pushing us to be a certain way. Today, let's pretend they don't exist.

What do you think society should focus less on? More on?

Discuss two things you would care less about, if you were free of the opinions of society.

2. Have you heard the 5 x 5 rule? If it isn't going to matter in 5 years, don't spend more than 5 minutes worrying about it. Not everything is going to apply to this concept, but perhaps a few things could.

Using the 5 x 5 rule, what is one worry you could let go of today?

What is something you've done recently that WILL matter in 5 years?

3. Reflection Day:

What are you grateful for today?

What was your favorite part of the day?

What are you looking forward to?

4. Make sure the people around you know what matters to you. That way they can support what is important to you.

How can you communicate your values to someone more clearly than you have in the past?

How has someone else supported what matters to you in the past?

5. We often let the opinions of others matter to us. We are social beings and it is hard not to take criticism to heart. Sometimes it is important to question the source of these opinions. Are they qualified to give said advice? Do they truly know what it is like to be in your position?

How have the opinions of others influenced your actions in the past?

Describe 5 things that matter most to you

Looking back 5 years, have any of these changed?

6. Check-in Day:

How are you doing?

What has been working out for you?

What changes have you noticed?

7. The most important lesson of this theme...YOU MATTER! Your feelings, thoughts, and everything about you matters. Remind yourself today that you matter and make yourself and your dreams a priority.

How do you remind yourself that you matter?

What can you do today to let yourself know you mean A LOT!

Theme 39:
All the Small Things

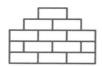

We are afraid to take on something huge because of how long it will take. Time passes whether we are working towards something or not. During this theme, start small on something big you've been wanting to accomplish.

1. Changing your life doesn't start with a dramatic shift, it starts with consistent small ones.

What is the tiniest shift you could make right now?

How have you been consistent in keeping up a small change?

2. Little things add up and make a big difference.

What is a small thing you already do every day that makes a big difference?

Name two things in your life that you could improve with a small change:

3. Reflection Day:

What are you grateful for today?

What was your favorite part of the day?

What are you looking forward to?

4. "From a tiny spark may burst a mighty flame" -Dante

A simple smile can change someone's day.
What is a small joy that keeps you going?

Small changes aren't linear, they don't have to happen in a row.
How can you make your small changes sustainable?

5. Enjoy the little things in life because one day you will look back and realize they were the big things.

That one day is today. What is "that big thing" that comes to mind?

Appreciate the little things, but keep one eye on the bigger picture.
How can you stay motivated to do the mundane things while striving for a goal?

6. Check-in Day:

How are you doing?

What has been working out for you?

What changes have you noticed?

Theme 40:
Let's Get Weird

Sometimes we take everything so seriously and it takes a huge toll on our bodies. We forget how small we are, and equally our problems are. Do something "just because" during this theme. Make a funny face to yourself in the mirror, crank some music, and be bold because life can't always be serious.

1. Whatever makes you weird is probably your biggest asset

What does weird mean to you?

What about yourself or past self do you think is weird?

2. Weirdness is something we don't see often. It's unique. It's rare. Odd, but fascinating. Weird is something to look at, it automatically commands attention, therefore, it is powerful.

Supernatural or superpower? Name 2 ways you have seen weirdness lead to success.

How are you rare or different from others?

3. Reflection Day:

What are you grateful for today?

What was your favorite part of the day?

What are you looking forward to?

4. Let's face it, when we are being silly or weird, we are having more fun, and we could all use more of that in our lives.

How could you add more silliness to your day?

What is something in your life that you could take a little less seriously?

5. Here is your permission to stop trying to be like everyone else.

What is your favorite weirdness about yourself?

Reflect on a time when you felt too weird for a situation/person.

6. Check-in Day:

How are you doing?

What has been working out for you?

What changes have you noticed?

Theme 41:
What is Perfect?

Perfect is something we all at one point or another have strived for. Only we have the power to determine if it exists or not. We can look at everything as perfect or absolutely nothing. In this theme, we are going to define what perfect really looks like.

1. Let's define what perfect means to you

Is perfect something that can be achieved?

What comes to mind when you think of the word "perfect?"

What are some things or situations that you would describe as perfect?

2. There is no such thing as "the perfect time". This concept makes us wait to have children, hold off on starting a project, or perhaps deciding to skip on a huge opportunity. The truth is, there isn't a perfect time, but there is always a present moment you can take advantage of.

How have you waited for "the perfect time" in the past?

What are you putting off now because you are waiting for that perfect time?

3. Reflection Day:

What are you grateful for today?

What was your favorite part of the day?

What are you looking forward to?

4. The pressure for perfection is real. There are supposed moments in our life that are supposed to be "perfect." Our wedding day, our first kiss, or graduation day. As we know, this is not always the case. It is a let down when our reality comes up short of what we wanted.

Reflect on a time when your expectations were not met. Looking back, would you change anything about what happened, or change your expectations?

How can you prevent yourself from being let down in the future?

5. If you want to, you can decide right now that you are perfect. You can decide that there is nothing that needs to be changed, and you can be happy with exactly who and what you are.

How can you remind yourself today that you are perfect?

Describe three things you would never change about yourself

6. Check-in Day:

How are you doing?

What has been working out for you?

What changes have you noticed?

Theme 42:
The Beauty of Life

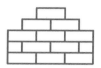

Life is beautiful. It sounds cliche and is not always the case. However, I want you to seek beauty in the most common places. Forget about what society says is beautiful; think of beauty as anything that captures your attention and makes you feel grateful.

1. Here's one we have all heard before, "Beauty is in the eye of the beholder" - Proverb. It is truly your sole opinion to decide if something is beautiful. Choose more things to classify as beautiful.

How have you limited your definition of beauty in the past?

What defines beauty for you today?

2. Beauty is not a feminine word. When you search beauty on the internet your results are going to be all aimed toward women. Despite the social standard, think of beauty as a genderless and limitless word. Look around you and make a conscious decision that it is beautiful.

In your immediate area, what can you find beauty in right now?

How can you practice seeing beauty in everyday things today?

3. Reflection Day:

What are you grateful for today?

```

```

What was your favorite part of the day?

```

```

What are you looking forward to?

```

```

4. Beauty is appreciating something for exactly the way it is. You are the observer.

What is something that is perfect just the way it is?

```

```

Think of something that others usually find unpleasant. Maybe sitting in traffic or taking out the trash. How can you find beauty in these scenarios?

```

```

5. Finding beauty in yourself. Loving who you are is a choice you must make everyday. Appreciating the marvelous things about yourself feels unnatural at first. We are told that we "should not be vain" and "caring about ourselves is selfish." Here is your permission to find beauty in your wonderful self.

Describe three beautiful things about yourself. Go beyond appearance.

What has made you feel beautiful in the past?

6. Check-in Day:

How are you doing?

What has been working out for you?

What changes have you noticed?

If you have any comments or questions about this workbook I would love to hear from you. You can find me at www.jennacarlton.life or email me at jennaleighcarlton@gmail.com